Life After Death

100 Quotes On The Journey After Death

Om Books International

First published in 2025

Om Books International

Corporate & Editorial Office
A-12, Sector 64, Noida 201 301
Uttar Pradesh, India
Phone: +91 120 477 4100
Email: editorial@ombooks.com
Website: www.ombooksinternational.com

Sales Office
107, Ansari Road, Darya Ganj,
New Delhi 110 002, India
Phone: +91 11 4000 9000
Email: sales@ombooks.com
Website: www.ombooks.com

ISBN: 978-93-63957-60-2

Printed in India

10 9 8 7 6 5 4 3 2 1

Death is the end of the physical body but the beginning of the soul's eternal existence.

Anonymous

Death is the final step in the journey of life, leading to an eternal home.

Anonymous

Death is a doorway to a new and eternal life.

Anonymous

To..

From..

Death is a
stripping away of
all that is not you.
The secret of life
is to 'die before
you die'
– and find that
there is no death.

Eckhart Tolle

To the
well-organized
mind, death is but
the next great
adventure.

J.K. Rowling

Death is nothing,
but
to live defeated
and inglorious
is to die daily.

Napoleon Bonaparte

Death is the passage to an eternal life filled with love and light.

Anonymous

Death is the final stage of life on earth, but the soul's journey continues in the afterlife.

Anonymous

Death is the end of the physical body, but the soul lives on.

Anonymous

Death is the doorway to a **new life**.

Anonymous

Death is the final frontier, but the soul goes beyond.

Anonymous

Death is but a transition from **this life to another.**

Anonymous

Death is but the next step in the grand adventure.

Anonymous

Death is the start
of a **new journey**
for the soul.

Anonymous

Death is the final adventure.

Anonymous

Death is the beginning of immortality.

Maximilien Robespierre

Death is the horizon, and the horizon is just the limit of our sight.

Anonymous

Death is the return to the origin of the soul.

Anonymous

Death is a new beginning for the soul.

Henry Ward Beecher

Death is the dropping of the flower that the fruit may swell.

Henry Ward Beecher

Death is only the end if you assume the story is about you.

Welcome to Night Vale

DEATH IS THE
ROAD TO AWE.

The Fountain

DEATH IS NOT THE
GREATEST LOSS IN LIFE.
THE GREATEST LOSS IS
WHAT DIES INSIDE US
WHILE WE LIVE.

Norman Cousins

Death is not the end, but a new beginning.

Anonymous

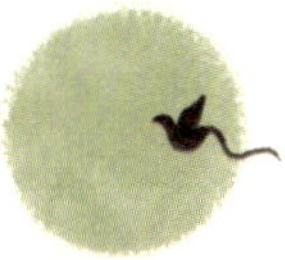

Death is the final chapter of life on earth, but the soul's journey continues.

Anonymous

Death is the end of a chapter, not the end of the book.

Anonymous

Death is not the
opposite of life,
but a part of it.

Haruki Murakami

Death is not the end.
It is the beginning of
a new chapter.

Anonymous

Death is just another journey to another place.

Anonymous

The life of the dead is placed in the memory of the living.

Marcus Tullius Cicero

Death is a natural part of life. Rejoice for those around you who transform into the Force.

Yoda

Those we love
never truly
leave us.
There are
things that
death cannot
touch.

J.K. Rowling

DEATH IS BUT A DOORWAY TO ANOTHER DIMENSION.

Anonymous

Death is nothing else but going home to God, the bond of love will be unbroken for all eternity.

Mother Teresa

**DO NOT FEAR DEATH,
BUT RATHER THE
UNLIVED LIFE.
YOU DON'T HAVE TO
LIVE FOREVER;
YOU JUST
HAVE TO LIVE.**

Natalie Babbitt

I do not fear death.
I had been dead
for billions and
billions of years
before I was born
and had not suffered
the slightest
inconvenience
from it.

Mark Twain

Death is just another stage of life, although the one you kind of hope comes last.

John Milton

Our dead
are never
dead to us,
until we have
forgotten
them.

George Eliot

Death is the golden key that opens the palace of eternity.

John Milton

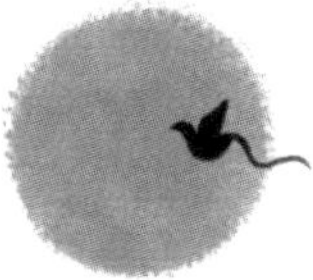

DEATH IS THE ULTIMATE AWAKENING.

Anonymous

DEATH IS THE CONTINUATION OF LIFE... IT IS ONLY A DIMENSION CHANGE.

Edgar Cayce

DEATH IS THE LAST CHAPTER IN TIME, BUT THE FIRST CHAPTER IN ETERNITY.

Anonymous

Death is a part of life, and it leads to the continuation of the soul's journey.

Anonymous

DEATH IS THE DOORWAY TO A NEW EXISTENCE BEYOND OUR PHYSICAL WORLD.

Anonymous

Death is not the end, but a passage to another realm.

Anonymous

Death is just a stepping stone to a beautiful life beyond.

Anonymous

DEATH IS THE BEGINNING OF THE SOUL'S NEXT JOURNEY.

Anonymous

To die is
poignantly bitter,
but the idea of
having to
die without
having lived is
unbearable.

Erich Fromm

DEATH IS THE STARLIT STRIP BETWEEN THE COMPANIONSHIP OF YESTERDAY AND THE REUNION OF TOMORROW.

Mark Twain

The bitterest tears shed over graves are for words left unsaid and deeds left undone.

Harriet Beecher Stowe

Death is but
a transition
from this life
to another
existence.

Edgar Cayce

Death is the gateway to life.

St. Francis of Assisi

The soul takes flight to the world that is invisible, and there arriving she is sure of bliss and forever dwells in paradise.

Plato

After your death, you will be what you were before your birth.

Arthur Schopenhauer

DEATH IS THE FINAL
WAKE-UP CALL.

Douglas Horton

I think of
death as some
delightful journey
that I shall take
when all my tasks
are done.

Ella Wheeler Wilcox

DEATH IS BUT A DOOR, TIME IS BUT A WINDOW. I'LL BE BACK!

Ghostbusters II

Death is just another step on the path to eternal life.

Anonymous

The soul never dies, but transforms from one life to another.

Plato

Death leaves a
heartache
no one can heal,
love leaves a
memory no one
can steal.

Irish Proverb

There is no death, only a change of worlds.

Chief Seattle

The soul is born old
but grows young.
That is the
comedy of life.
The body is born
young and grows old.
That is life's tragedy.

Oscar Wilde

What we have once enjoyed we can never lose. All that we love deeply becomes a part of us.

Helen Keller

Death ends a life,
not a relationship.

Mitch Albom

The soul takes
nothing with her to
the next world but
her education and
her culture.

Plato

Death is the gateway to eternal life.

Anonymous

Death is the end of the body's journey, but the soul continues on.

Anonymous

While we are
mourning the loss
of our friend, others
are rejoicing to
meet him
behind the veil.

John Taylor

TO DIE WILL BE AN AWFULLY BIG ADVENTURE.

J.M. Barrie

Death is a transition to a higher plane of existence.

Anonymous

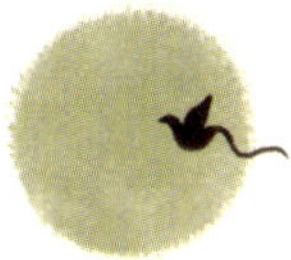

Death is the start of a new journey in the afterlife.

Anonymous

The energy of
the soul cannot
be destroyed by
death.

Bhagavad Gita

The day which we fear as our last is but the birthday of eternity.

Seneca

The journey
doesn't end here.
Death is just
another path,
one that we all
must take.

J.R.R. Tolkien

He who has
gone, so we
but cherish his
memory, abides
with us, more
potent, nay,
more present
than the living
man.

Antoine de Saint-Exupéry

THEY THAT LOVE BEYOND THE WORLD CANNOT BE SEPARATED BY IT. DEATH CANNOT KILL WHAT NEVER DIES.

William Penn

LIFE AND DEATH ARE ONE THREAD, THE SAME LINE VIEWED FROM DIFFERENT SIDES.

Lao Tzu

The dead never truly die. They simply change form.

Anonymous

I am not afraid
of death,
I just don't want to be
there when it happens.

Woody Allen

Death is not the end. There remains the litigation over the estate.

Ambrose Bierce

Death is a challenge.
It tells us
not to waste time...
It tells us to tell
each other right
now that we love
each other.

Leo Buscaglia

WE ALL DIE.
THE GOAL ISN'T TO
LIVE FOREVER, THE
GOAL IS TO CREATE
SOMETHING THAT
WILL.

Chuck Palahniuk

Death is but crossing the world, as friends do the seas; they live in one another still.

William Penn

To live in hearts we leave behind is not to die.

Thomas Campbell

Goodbyes are only for those who love with their eyes. Because for those who love with heart and soul, there is no such thing as separation.

Rumi

Death is but a stepping stone to a new reality.

Anonymous

Death is the transition to an everlasting life.

Anonymous

THE FEAR
OF DEATH
FOLLOWS
FROM THE
FEAR OF LIFE.
A MAN WHO
LIVES FULLY
IS PREPARED
TO DIE AT
ANY TIME.

Mark Twain

For life and death
are one,
even as the river
and the sea
are one.

Khalil Gibran

YOU NEED TO BE GREEDY OR IGNORANT TO TRULY WANT TO LIVE FOREVER.

Mokokoma Mokhonoana

Death is a journey into the unknown, but the soul is eternal.

Anonymous

FOR DEATH IS NO MORE THAN A TURNING OF US OVER FROM TIME TO ETERNITY.

William Penn

Death may be the greatest of all human blessings.

Socrates

I BELIEVE THAT
WHEN DEATH
CLOSES OUR EYES
WE SHALL AWAKEN
TO A LIGHT, OF
WHICH OUR
SUNLIGHT IS BUT
THE SHADOW.

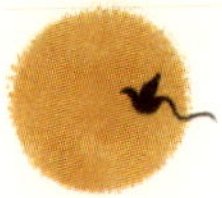

Arthur Schopenhauer

Death is
a new
adventure in
existence.

Franklin D. Roosevelt

Death is nature's way of telling you to slow down.

Dick Sharples

The soul never takes birth and never dies at any time nor does it come into being again when the body is created. The soul is birthless, eternal, imperishable, and timeless.

Bhagavad Gita

DEATH IS NOT THE END, BUT THE BEGINNING OF A NEW LIFE.

Osho

DEATH IS NOT
EXTINGUISHING
THE LIGHT;
IT IS PUTTING OUT
THE LAMP
BECAUSE THE
DAWN HAS COME.

Rabindranath Tagore

Our death is but a sleep and a remembering.

William Wordsworth